301
things to

301
things to

WR
ITE

BY BROOKE KUNZ

BUSHEL
& PECK
BOOKS™

1

YOUR BEST FRIEND JUST TURNED INTO A FISH! WHAT DO YOU DO NOW?

_____

_____

_____

_____

_____

_____

_____

_____

_____

_____

_____

_____

_____

_____

WHAT WOULD YOUR PET SAY IF IT COULD TALK?

_____

_____

_____

_____

_____

_____

_____

_____

_____

_____

_____

_____

_____

_____

WHAT WOULD YOU DO IF YOU WERE PRESIDENT FOR A DAY?

_____

_____

_____

_____

_____

_____

_____

_____

_____

_____

_____

_____

_____

_____

_____

_____

WHAT WOULD HAPPEN IF PIGS *COULD* FLY?

_____

_____

_____

_____

_____

_____

_____

_____

_____

_____

_____

_____

_____

_____

_____

HOW DID THE COW JUMP OVER THE MOON?

6

**IF YOU COULD CREATE A NEW HOLIDAY,
WHAT WOULD IT BE?**

WHERE WOULD YOU GO IF YOU COULD BECOME INVISIBLE?

IF YOU COULD BECOME ANY CARTOON CHARACTER FOR ONE DAY, WHO WOULD YOU BE? WHY?

WHAT IS THE FUNNIEST SOUND IN THE WORLD? WHAT DOES IT SOUND LIKE?

_____

_____

_____

_____

_____

_____

_____

_____

_____

_____

_____

_____

_____

_____

_____

10

INVENT A CRAZY, NEW OLYMPIC SPORT AND DESCRIBE IT!

11

WHAT IF THERE WERE NO GRAVITY ON EARTH?

_____

_____

_____

_____

_____

_____

_____

_____

_____

_____

_____

_____

_____

_____

_____

_____

_____

12

WHAT'S THE WEIRDEST DREAM YOU'VE EVER HAD?

_____

_____

_____

_____

_____

_____

_____

_____

_____

_____

_____

_____

_____

YOUR DOG HOPPED ON THE SCHOOL BUS!
WHAT HAPPENS NEXT?

14

WHAT IF THE SKY WERE PINK?

_____

_____

_____

_____

_____

_____

_____

_____

_____

_____

_____

_____

_____

_____

_____

15

YOU'RE WEARING A BATHING SUIT IN A SNOW STORM. WHAT HAPPENS NEXT?

_____

_____

_____

_____

_____

_____

_____

_____

_____

_____

_____

_____

_____

_____

_____

_____

16

WHAT IF YOUR DAY HAPPENED IN REVERSE?

_____

_____

_____

_____

_____

_____

_____

_____

_____

_____

_____

_____

_____

_____

_____

_____

DESCRIBE THE BRAVEST THING YOU'VE EVER DONE.

18

TELL ABOUT A CITY MADE ENTIRELY OF CANDY.

_____

_____

_____

_____

_____

_____

_____

_____

_____

_____

_____

_____

_____

_____

WHERE IS THE END OF THE RAINBOW?

20

WHAT'S THE BEST WAY TO CATCH A LEPRECHAUN?

_____

_____

_____

_____

_____

_____

_____

_____

_____

_____

_____

_____

_____

_____

21

IF YOU HAD A PARROT, WHAT WOULD IT SAY?

_____

_____

_____

_____

_____

_____

_____

_____

_____

_____

_____

_____

_____

_____

HOW WOULD A LAUGHING MACHINE WORK?

_____

_____

_____

_____

_____

_____

_____

_____

_____

_____

_____

_____

_____

_____

WHAT IF MONEY *REALLY* GREW ON TREES?

_____

_____

_____

_____

_____

_____

_____

_____

_____

_____

_____

_____

_____

_____

WHICH WILD ANIMAL WOULD MAKE THE BEST PET?

_____

_____

_____

_____

_____

_____

_____

_____

_____

_____

_____

_____

_____

_____

DESCRIBE A CAMERA THAT CAPTURES . . . SMELLS!

_____

_____

_____

_____

_____

_____

_____

_____

_____

_____

_____

_____

_____

_____

26

WRITE ABOUT YOUR ADVENTURES ON A MOUNTAIN
MADE OF SPAGHETTI.

_____

_____

_____

_____

_____

_____

_____

_____

_____

_____

_____

_____

_____

_____

WHAT WOULD LIFE BE LIKE IF YOU WERE AN OCTOPUS?

_____

_____

_____

_____

_____

_____

_____

_____

_____

_____

_____

_____

_____

_____

_____

_____

WHAT IF YOU LIVED IN A MANSION MADE OF JELLO?

_____

_____

_____

_____

_____

_____

_____

_____

_____

_____

_____

_____

_____

WRITE ABOUT SOME FRIENDLY ALIENS WHO VISITED EARTH LAST WEEK.

30

WHAT'S THE LUCKIEST THING THAT HAS EVER HAPPENED TO YOU?

_____

_____

_____

_____

_____

_____

_____

_____

_____

_____

_____

_____

_____

_____

WHAT WOULD YOU DO WITH A MILLION DOLLARS?

_____

_____

_____

_____

_____

_____

_____

_____

_____

_____

_____

_____

_____

_____

_____

_____

32

DESCRIBE AN AMUSEMENT PARK THAT'S NEVER EXISTED.

_____

_____

_____

_____

_____

_____

_____

_____

_____

_____

_____

_____

_____

_____

WHAT ARE DANCE PARTIES LIKE ON THE MOON?

34

WHAT HAPPENED TO THE *FOURTH* LITTLE PIG?

_____

_____

_____

_____

_____

_____

_____

_____

_____

_____

_____

_____

_____

_____

INVENT A NEW FLAVOR OF ICE CREAM.

_____

_____

_____

_____

_____

_____

_____

_____

_____

_____

_____

_____

_____

WHAT IF YOU NEVER GOT OLDER?

_____

_____

_____

_____

_____

_____

_____

_____

_____

_____

_____

_____

_____

_____

_____

WHAT'S THE COOLEST PLACE YOU'VE EVER VISITED?

_____

_____

_____

_____

_____

_____

_____

_____

_____

_____

_____

_____

_____

_____

_____

_____

_____

WHAT RULES WOULD YOU MAKE IF YOU
WERE THE TEACHER FOR A DAY?

_____

_____

_____

_____

_____

_____

_____

_____

_____

_____

_____

_____

_____

_____

_____

WHAT WILL THE WORLD BE LIKE WHEN YOU'RE AN ADULT?

_____

_____

_____

_____

_____

_____

_____

_____

_____

_____

_____

_____

_____

_____

_____

_____

40

WHAT'S THE BEST SUPERPOWER? WHY?

_____
_____
_____
_____
_____
_____
_____
_____
_____
_____
_____
_____
_____
_____

41

WHAT IF DRAGONS BREATHED ICE INSTEAD OF FIRE?

_____

_____

_____

_____

_____

_____

_____

_____

_____

_____

_____

_____

_____

_____

_____

_____

IF YOU WERE KING OR QUEEN, WHAT WOULD YOUR CASTLE LOOK LIKE?

_____

_____

_____

_____

_____

_____

_____

_____

_____

_____

_____

_____

_____

_____

43

DESCRIBE A TIME WHEN YOU MADE PEOPLE LAUGH.

WRITE A NEW KNOCK-KNOCK JOKE.

_____

_____

_____

_____

_____

_____

_____

_____

_____

_____

_____

_____

_____

WHAT DO YOUR PETS DO WHEN NO ONE IS HOME?

TELL ABOUT A MAGICAL PENCIL THAT MAKES DRAWINGS COME TO LIFE.

_____

_____

_____

_____

_____

_____

_____

_____

_____

_____

_____

_____

_____

_____

WHAT MAGICAL CREATURES LIVE INSIDE VOLCANOES?

_____

_____

_____

_____

_____

_____

_____

_____

_____

_____

_____

_____

_____

_____

_____

WHERE DID THE CAT GET HIS HAT?

_____

_____

_____

_____

_____

_____

_____

_____

_____

_____

_____

_____

_____

_____

_____

WHAT IF ANIMALS COULD DRIVE?

_____

_____

_____

_____

_____

_____

_____

_____

_____

_____

_____

_____

_____

_____

_____

_____

_____

50

IF YOU WON AN AWARD FOR BEING THE BEST AT SOMETHING, WHAT WOULD IT BE?

_____

_____

_____

_____

_____

_____

_____

_____

_____

_____

_____

_____

_____

_____

51

WHAT DO GOLDFISH THINK ABOUT?

_____

_____

_____

_____

_____

_____

_____

_____

_____

_____

_____

_____

_____

_____

IF YOU GIVE A MOUSE A COOKIE, WHAT ELSE MIGHT HAPPEN NEXT?

_____

_____

_____

_____

_____

_____

_____

_____

_____

_____

_____

_____

_____

_____

53

DESCRIBE A CAKE THAT MAKES PEOPLE FLY.

_____

_____

_____

_____

_____

_____

_____

_____

_____

_____

_____

_____

_____

_____

HOW DO *YOU* THINK CAVEMEN
LEARNED TO MAKE FIRE?

55

WHAT ARE SOME OF THE FUNNIEST
WORDS YOU'VE EVER HEARD?

_____

_____

_____

_____

_____

_____

_____

_____

_____

_____

_____

_____

_____

_____

56

**WHAT WOULD YOU DO IF YOU NEVER
HAD TO GO TO SCHOOL?**

_____

_____

_____

_____

_____

_____

_____

_____

_____

_____

_____

_____

_____

_____

WRITE A STORY ABOUT A SUPERHERO WITH AN IRRATIONAL FEAR.

58

WHAT DO SANTA'S ELVES DO DURING THE SUMMER?

_____

_____

_____

_____

_____

_____

_____

_____

_____

_____

_____

_____

_____

_____

WHERE DO UNICORNS LIVE?

_____

_____

_____

_____

_____

_____

_____

_____

_____

_____

_____

_____

_____

_____

_____

60

WHERE DOES THE EASTER BUNNY GO ON VACATION?

_____

_____

_____

_____

_____

_____

_____

_____

_____

_____

_____

_____

_____

WHAT DOES THE TOOTH FAIRY DO WITH ALL THOSE TEETH?

_____

_____

_____

_____

_____

_____

_____

_____

_____

_____

_____

_____

_____

_____

62

WHY DID THE CHICKEN *REALLY* CROSS THE ROAD?

_____

_____

_____

_____

_____

_____

_____

_____

_____

_____

_____

_____

_____

_____

WRITE ABOUT A TIME YOU JOINED PIRATES ON A HUNT FOR SUNKEN TREASURE.

_____

_____

_____

_____

_____

_____

_____

_____

_____

_____

_____

_____

_____

_____

64

WHAT IF HUMANS HAD EYES ON THE
BACKS OF THEIR HEAD?

_____

_____

_____

_____

_____

_____

_____

_____

_____

_____

_____

_____

_____

_____

WHAT IF YOU COULD READ MINDS?

_____

_____

_____

_____

_____

_____

_____

_____

_____

_____

_____

_____

_____

_____

_____

_____

66

**TELL ABOUT A CLOWN WHO
COULDN'T STOP CRYING.**

WHAT IF HUMANS COULD WALK ON CLOUDS?

_____

_____

_____

_____

_____

_____

_____

_____

_____

_____

_____

_____

_____

_____

_____

_____

WHAT CRAZY CLOTHES WILL PEOPLE
WEAR IN THE FUTURE?

_____

_____

_____

_____

_____

_____

_____

_____

_____

_____

_____

_____

_____

_____

WHAT WOULD HAPPEN IF YOU WERE
LEFT HOME ALONE?

_____

_____

_____

_____

_____

_____

_____

_____

_____

_____

_____

_____

_____

_____

70

**WHAT DO YOU HOPE ROBOTS WILL BE ABLE
TO DO IN THE FUTURE?**

_____

_____

_____

_____

_____

_____

_____

_____

_____

_____

_____

_____

_____

**DESCRIBE THE NEW PLANET YOU DISCOVERED
ON A RECENT SPACE VOYAGE.**

_____

_____

_____

_____

_____

_____

_____

_____

_____

_____

_____

_____

_____

_____

WRITE A COMMERCIAL FOR YOUR FAVORITE CEREAL.

_____

_____

_____

_____

_____

_____

_____

_____

_____

_____

_____

_____

_____

_____

73

WHAT IF YOUR SHADOW RAN AWAY FROM YOU?

_____

_____

_____

_____

_____

_____

_____

_____

_____

_____

_____

_____

_____

_____

74

WHO WOULD YOU LIKE TO TRADE PLACES WITH FOR A DAY? WHY?

_____

_____

_____

_____

_____

_____

_____

_____

_____

_____

_____

_____

_____

_____

DESCRIBE THE BEST SUMMER VACATION EVER.

_____

_____

_____

_____

_____

_____

_____

_____

_____

_____

_____

_____

_____

_____

WHAT WOULD YOU DO IF A SPACESHIP LANDED IN YOUR BACKYARD?

WRITE ABOUT A SCIENCE EXPERIMENT
GONE WRONG.

_____

_____

_____

_____

_____

_____

_____

_____

_____

_____

_____

_____

_____

_____

_____

WHAT IF YOU SNEEZED COTTON CANDY?

_____

_____

_____

_____

_____

_____

_____

_____

_____

_____

_____

_____

_____

_____

WHICH MOVIE DO YOU WISH YOU COULD LIVE IN? WHY?

_____

_____

_____

_____

_____

_____

_____

_____

_____

_____

_____

_____

_____

_____

80

WHAT WOULD YOU DO IF YOU GOT TRAPPED IN THE ZOO FOR THE NIGHT?

_____

_____

_____

_____

_____

_____

_____

_____

_____

_____

_____

_____

_____

DESCRIBE A WORLD WHERE IT SNOWS EVERY DAY.

_____

_____

_____

_____

_____

_____

_____

_____

_____

_____

_____

_____

_____

_____

_____

HOW DO MONSTERS GET UNDER THE BED?

_____

_____

_____

_____

_____

_____

_____

_____

_____

_____

_____

_____

_____

_____

_____

HOW WILL YOU SUCCESSFULLY COMPLETE YOUR SECRET SPY MISSION?

WHAT WOULD YOU RE-NAME SNOW WHITE'S SEVEN DWARFS?

_____

_____

_____

_____

_____

_____

_____

_____

_____

_____

_____

_____

_____

_____

WHAT WOULD HAPPEN IF A DINOSAUR WAS SET LOOSE IN YOUR CITY?

_____

_____

_____

_____

_____

_____

_____

_____

_____

_____

_____

_____

_____

_____

_____

WHAT WOULD YOU DO IF YOU FOUND A
MERMAID IN YOUR BATHTUB?

_____

_____

_____

_____

_____

_____

_____

_____

_____

_____

_____

_____

_____

_____

WHO IS JOHN JACOB JINGLEHEIMER SCHMIDT?

_____

_____

_____

_____

_____

_____

_____

_____

_____

_____

_____

_____

_____

_____

88

WHAT WILL LIFE BE LIKE 200 YEARS FROM NOW?

_____

_____

_____

_____

_____

_____

_____

_____

_____

_____

_____

_____

_____

_____

INVENT A NEW DAY OF THE WEEK.

WHAT'S THE WEIRDEST FOOD YOU'VE EVER EATEN? DESCRIBE WHAT IT TASTED LIKE.

_____

_____

_____

_____

_____

_____

_____

_____

_____

_____

_____

_____

_____

_____

**WRITE ABOUT A TIME WHEN IT SNOWED
IN THE SUMMER.**

_____

_____

_____

_____

_____

_____

_____

_____

_____

_____

_____

_____

_____

_____

92

WHAT'S THE MOST AMAZING TOY ANYONE COULD EVER GIVE YOU?

_____

_____

_____

_____

_____

_____

_____

_____

_____

_____

_____

_____

_____

**WRITE A SPOOKY STORY TO TELL
AROUND THE CAMPFIRE.**

_____

_____

_____

_____

_____

_____

_____

_____

_____

_____

_____

_____

_____

_____

_____

_____

_____

WHAT IF YOU WERE A GHOST?

_____

_____

_____

_____

_____

_____

_____

_____

_____

_____

_____

_____

_____

_____

WHAT'S A SILLY AWARD YOU'D BE SURE TO WIN?

WHAT IF CINDERELLA NEVER LOST HER SHOE?

_____

_____

_____

_____

_____

_____

_____

_____

_____

_____

_____

_____

_____

_____

**TELL A STORY ABOUT DIGGING A HOLE
ALL THE WAY TO CHINA.**

WHAT IF YOU JUST MET THE TWIN YOU DIDN'T KNOW YOU HAD?

_____

_____

_____

_____

_____

_____

_____

_____

_____

_____

_____

_____

_____

_____

_____

WRITE ABOUT A REALLY BORING SUPERPOWER.

_____

_____

_____

_____

_____

_____

_____

_____

_____

_____

_____

_____

_____

_____

_____

_____

DESCRIBE WHAT IT WOULD BE LIKE TO GO ON A TRIP WITH SOMEONE WHO CAN'T STOP TALKING.

101

HOW COULD YOU MAKE A MILLION DOLLARS
TOMORROW?

_____

_____

_____

_____

_____

_____

_____

_____

_____

_____

_____

_____

_____

_____

**IF YOU COULD PLAN A CLASS FIELD TRIP,
WHERE WOULD YOU GO?**

_____

_____

_____

_____

_____

_____

_____

_____

_____

_____

_____

_____

_____

_____

IF YOU HAD TO WEAR THE SAME CLOTHES EVERY DAY, WHAT WOULD YOU WEAR?

_____

_____

_____

_____

_____

_____

_____

_____

_____

_____

_____

_____

_____

_____

_____

WRITE A STORY WITHOUT USING THE WORD "AND."

_____

_____

_____

_____

_____

_____

_____

_____

_____

_____

_____

_____

_____

_____

_____

_____

WHAT FAMOUS PERSON DO YOU WANT TO BE BEST FRIENDS WITH? WHY?

_____

_____

_____

_____

_____

_____

_____

_____

_____

_____

_____

_____

_____

_____

_____

_____

WHAT IF YOU HAD TO LIVE IN A HAMSTER CAGE?

_____

_____

_____

_____

_____

_____

_____

_____

_____

_____

_____

_____

_____

_____

WHAT WOULD YOU DO ON A TRIP TO MARS?

_____

_____

_____

_____

_____

_____

_____

_____

_____

_____

_____

_____

_____

_____

_____

WHAT IF YOU COULD FLY?

_____

_____

_____

_____

_____

_____

_____

_____

_____

_____

_____

_____

_____

_____

WHAT WOULD YOU DO IF YOUR PARENTS TURNED INTO KIDS OVERNIGHT?

_____

_____

_____

_____

_____

_____

_____

_____

_____

_____

_____

_____

_____

_____

_____

_____

110

WRITE ABOUT A TIME YOU LAUGHED
UNTIL YOU CRIED.

_____

_____

_____

_____

_____

_____

_____

_____

_____

_____

_____

_____

_____

**WHERE WOULD YOU GO IF YOU DISCOVERED
A TIME MACHINE?**

_____

_____

_____

_____

_____

_____

_____

_____

_____

_____

_____

_____

_____

_____

**DESCRIBE A TIME WHEN IT RAINED
CHOCOLATE MILK.**

_____

_____

_____

_____

_____

_____

_____

_____

_____

_____

_____

_____

_____

_____

WHAT WOULD HAPPEN IF THE GARBAGE MAN NEVER CAME AGAIN?

_____

_____

_____

_____

_____

_____

_____

_____

_____

_____

_____

_____

_____

_____

DESCRIBE THE MOST EPIC BIRTHDAY PARTY EVER.

_____

_____

_____

_____

_____

_____

_____

_____

_____

_____

_____

_____

_____

_____

115

IMAGINE THERE ARE CHARACTERS IN YOUR BRAIN WHO ACT OUT YOUR DREAMS. WHAT DO THEY DO?

_____

_____

_____

_____

_____

_____

_____

_____

_____

_____

_____

_____

_____

_____

**WRITE ABOUT A MAILBOX THAT TRANSPORTS YOU TO
AN ALTERNATE UNIVERSE.**

_____

_____

_____

_____

_____

_____

_____

_____

_____

_____

_____

_____

_____

_____

WHAT IF YOU WORE SHOES ON YOUR HEAD
AND HATS ON YOUR FEET?

_____

_____

_____

_____

_____

_____

_____

_____

_____

_____

_____

_____

_____

_____

WHAT DO DOLPHINS SAY TO EACH OTHER?

_____

_____

_____

_____

_____

_____

_____

_____

_____

_____

_____

_____

_____

DESCRIBE A RACE FOR SNAILS.

WRITE ABOUT A ROCK BAND THAT USES THEIR ARMPITS AS INSTRUMENTS.

_____

_____

_____

_____

_____

_____

_____

_____

_____

_____

_____

_____

_____

_____

WHAT FOODS WOULD YOU EAT IF YOU WERE ON A ROCKET SHIP?

_____

_____

_____

_____

_____

_____

_____

_____

_____

_____

_____

_____

_____

_____

_____

WHAT WOULD HAPPEN IF YOU TURNED INTO A TOY?

_____

_____

_____

_____

_____

_____

_____

_____

_____

_____

_____

_____

_____

_____

TELL ABOUT THE GOAT THAT ATE EVERY
BOOK IN THE LIBRARY.

_____

_____

_____

_____

_____

_____

_____

_____

_____

_____

_____

_____

_____

_____

**WRITE ABOUT A KID WHO TURNED ORANGE FROM
EATING TOO MANY CARROTS.**

_____

_____

_____

_____

_____

_____

_____

_____

_____

_____

_____

_____

_____

_____

_____

MAKE UP A STORY ABOUT THE GIANT IN THE SKY WHO CAUSES LIGHTNING STORMS.

WHAT'S THE WEIRDEST THING YOU COULD PUT PEANUT BUTTER ON?

_____

_____

_____

_____

_____

_____

_____

_____

_____

_____

_____

_____

_____

_____

WHAT IF YOU HAD THE HEARING OF A DOG?

_____

_____

_____

_____

_____

_____

_____

_____

_____

_____

_____

_____

_____

_____

_____

128

WHAT IF YOU SLEPT HANGING UPSIDE-DOWN,
LIKE A BAT?

_____

_____

_____

_____

_____

_____

_____

_____

_____

_____

_____

_____

_____

_____

WHAT DOES IT MEAN IF YOU HAVE A DREAM ABOUT YOUR TEETH FALLING OUT?

130

**TELL A STORY ABOUT YOUR AWARD-WINNING
VEGETABLE AT THE COUNTY FAIR.**

_____

_____

_____

_____

_____

_____

_____

_____

_____

_____

_____

_____

_____

WRITE A NEW BIRTHDAY SONG.

_____

_____

_____

_____

_____

_____

_____

_____

_____

_____

_____

_____

_____

_____

**WHY SHOULD YOU BE HIRED TO JOIN
A TRAVELING CIRCUS?**

_____

_____

_____

_____

_____

_____

_____

_____

_____

_____

_____

_____

_____

_____

IMAGINE YOU CHANGED COLORS
DEPENDING ON YOUR MOOD.

_____

_____

_____

_____

_____

_____

_____

_____

_____

_____

_____

_____

_____

_____

WHAT IS AT THE BOTTOM OF THE OCEAN?

_____

_____

_____

_____

_____

_____

_____

_____

_____

_____

_____

_____

_____

INVENT A NEW KIND OF ALARM CLOCK.
WHAT MAKES IT DIFFERENT?

_____

_____

_____

_____

_____

_____

_____

_____

_____

_____

_____

_____

_____

_____

_____

WHAT IF YOUR NOSE GREW WHEN YOU TOLD A LIE?

_____

_____

_____

_____

_____

_____

_____

_____

_____

_____

_____

_____

_____

_____

_____

137

WHAT IF YOU COULD SEE SMELLS AND HEAR COLORS?

_____

_____

_____

_____

_____

_____

_____

_____

_____

_____

_____

_____

_____

_____

_____

_____

WRITE ABOUT A SURFING TRIP TO ANTARCTICA.

_____

_____

_____

_____

_____

_____

_____

_____

_____

_____

_____

_____

_____

_____

_____

**WHAT IF YOU SLEPT DURING THE DAY
AND STAYED AWAKE AT NIGHT?**

WHAT AGE WOULD YOU LIKE TO BE FOREVER? WHY?

_____

_____

_____

_____

_____

_____

_____

_____

_____

_____

_____

_____

_____

_____

WHAT IF YOU NEVER GREW UP?

_____

_____

_____

_____

_____

_____

_____

_____

_____

_____

_____

_____

_____

_____

_____

**TELL ABOUT A FISH WHO WAS BEST FRIENDS
WITH A SHARK.**

_____

_____

_____

_____

_____

_____

_____

_____

_____

_____

_____

_____

_____

_____

WHICH *DID* COME FIRST:
THE CHICKEN OR THE EGG?

_____

_____

_____

_____

_____

_____

_____

_____

_____

_____

_____

_____

_____

_____

_____

_____

WRITE ABOUT A DENTIST FOR CROCODILES.

_____

_____

_____

_____

_____

_____

_____

_____

_____

_____

_____

_____

_____

WHAT'S THE FUNNIEST EXCUSE FOR NOT DOING YOUR HOMEWORK?

DESCRIBE A TIME YOU WENT SKYDIVING AND YOUR PARACHUTE DIDN'T WORK.

_____

_____

_____

_____

_____

_____

_____

_____

_____

_____

_____

_____

_____

_____

_____

WHAT WOULD YOU DO IF YOU SHRANK
TO THE SIZE OF AN ANT?

_____

_____

_____

_____

_____

_____

_____

_____

_____

_____

_____

_____

_____

_____

_____

WRITE ABOUT A TURTLE WHO DIDN'T HAVE A SHELL.

_____

_____

_____

_____

_____

_____

_____

_____

_____

_____

_____

_____

_____

_____

WHAT WOULD YOU DO IF YOU HAD
SUPERHUMAN STRENGTH?

WHAT'S THE WACKIEST SANDWICH YOU CAN IMAGINE EATING?

WHERE WOULD YOU GO IN A HOT AIR BALLOON?

_____

_____

_____

_____

_____

_____

_____

_____

_____

_____

_____

_____

_____

_____

WHAT IF YOU TOOK YOUR PET FISH FOR A WALK?

_____

_____

_____

_____

_____

_____

_____

_____

_____

_____

_____

_____

_____

_____

WRITE ABOUT A BOWLING ALLEY THAT USES
WATERMELONS INSTEAD OF BOWLING BALLS.

_____

_____

_____

_____

_____

_____

_____

_____

_____

_____

_____

_____

_____

_____

_____

TELL ABOUT A PIG WHO LOVED TO BE CLEAN.

_____

_____

_____

_____

_____

_____

_____

_____

_____

_____

_____

_____

_____

IMAGINE A FARM THAT GREW SOMETHING BESIDES PLANTS.

IF YOU STARTED YOUR OWN COMPANY,
WHAT WOULD IT BE?

IF YOU WENT INTO A COCOON LIKE A BUTTERFLY, WHAT MIGHT YOU TURN INTO?

_____

_____

_____

_____

_____

_____

_____

_____

_____

_____

_____

_____

_____

_____

_____

_____

WHAT IF BIGFOOT IS REAL?

_____

_____

_____

_____

_____

_____

_____

_____

_____

_____

_____

_____

_____

_____

_____

WHAT IF YOU WERE THE SMARTEST PERSON
IN THE WORLD?

_____

_____

_____

_____

_____

_____

_____

_____

_____

_____

_____

_____

_____

_____

_____

_____

**YOU'RE WEARING A SNOWSUIT AT THE BEACH.
WHAT HAPPENS NEXT?**

HOW DID ZEBRAS GET THEIR STRIPES?

_____

_____

_____

_____

_____

_____

_____

_____

_____

_____

_____

_____

_____

_____

_____

_____

WHAT WOULD CAVEMEN THINK ABOUT THE WORLD TODAY?

_____

_____

_____

_____

_____

_____

_____

_____

_____

_____

_____

_____

_____

_____

WHAT WOULD YOU DO IF YOU HAD X-RAY VISION?

_____

_____

_____

_____

_____

_____

_____

_____

_____

_____

_____

_____

_____

_____

_____

WHAT WILL YOU BE DOING ON THIS DAY
FIVE YEARS FROM NOW?

IS THE GLASS HALF-EMPTY OR HALF-FULL?

_____

_____

_____

_____

_____

_____

_____

_____

_____

_____

_____

_____

_____

_____

WHAT IF A TORNADO TOOK YOUR HOUSE TO THE TOP OF MOUNT EVEREST?

_____

_____

_____

_____

_____

_____

_____

_____

_____

_____

_____

_____

_____

_____

_____

WHAT'S ONE THING YOU WISH A DRONE COULD DELIVER TO YOUR HOUSE TOMORROW?

_____

_____

_____

_____

_____

_____

_____

_____

_____

_____

_____

_____

_____

_____

WRITE A STORY ABOUT OPPOSITE DAY.

WHAT IF HUMANS NEVER BLINKED?

WHO DO YOU WISH COULD SUBSTITUTE TEACH YOUR CLASS FOR A DAY?

_____

_____

_____

_____

_____

_____

_____

_____

_____

_____

_____

_____

_____

_____

_____

WHAT IF ELEPHANTS WERE THE SIZE OF ANTS?

_____

_____

_____

_____

_____

_____

_____

_____

_____

_____

_____

_____

_____

_____

_____

WHAT'S SOMETHING BIG THAT YOU WISH COULD FIT IN YOUR POCKET?

_____

_____

_____

_____

_____

_____

_____

_____

_____

_____

_____

_____

_____

_____

WHAT IF A CAT RAN FOR PRESIDENT?

_____

_____

_____

_____

_____

_____

_____

_____

_____

_____

_____

_____

_____

_____

_____

174

WHAT IF LIONS WERE VEGETARIANS?

_____

_____

_____

_____

_____

_____

_____

_____

_____

_____

_____

_____

_____

_____

HOW DID THE EASTER BUNNY GET HIS JOB?

_____

_____

_____

_____

_____

_____

_____

_____

_____

_____

_____

_____

_____

**IF YOU COULD INVENT A NEW KIND OF CAR,
WHAT WOULD IT BE LIKE?**

WHAT WOULD THE TOOTH FAIRY DO IF KIDS NEVER LOST THEIR TEETH?

_____

_____

_____

_____

_____

_____

_____

_____

_____

_____

_____

_____

_____

_____

DESCRIBE A WORLD WHERE EVERY DAY IS SUMMER.

_____

_____

_____

_____

_____

_____

_____

_____

_____

_____

_____

_____

_____

_____

_____

WHAT DO GIANTS EAT FOR BREAKFAST?

_____

_____

_____

_____

_____

_____

_____

_____

_____

_____

_____

_____

_____

WHAT IF YOU COULD ONLY WALK BACKWARDS?

_____

_____

_____

_____

_____

_____

_____

_____

_____

_____

_____

_____

_____

_____

_____

WHAT IF THE WORLD WAS UPSIDE-DOWN?

_____

_____

_____

_____

_____

_____

_____

_____

_____

_____

_____

_____

_____

_____

WHAT WILL GROW FROM THE MYSTERIOUS SEED YOU JUST PLANTED?

_____

_____

_____

_____

_____

_____

_____

_____

_____

_____

_____

_____

_____

_____

HOW WOULD YOU SURVIVE A ZOMBIE ATTACK?

_____

_____

_____

_____

_____

_____

_____

_____

_____

_____

_____

_____

_____

_____

_____

IF YOU EXPERIENCED THE WORLD'S BIGGEST EARTHQUAKE, WHAT WOULD HAPPEN AFTER?

_____

_____

_____

_____

_____

_____

_____

_____

_____

_____

_____

_____

_____

_____

HOW DO BABY BIRDS LEARN TO FLY?

_____

_____

_____

_____

_____

_____

_____

_____

_____

_____

_____

_____

_____

_____

**HOW WOULD YOU PASS THE TIME IF YOU HAD TO
COUNT TO A BILLION?**

_____

_____

_____

_____

_____

_____

_____

_____

_____

_____

_____

_____

_____

_____

WHAT IF YOU COULD BREATHE UNDERWATER?

_____

_____

_____

_____

_____

_____

_____

_____

_____

_____

_____

_____

_____

_____

188

WRITE A RHYME ABOUT YOUR FAMILY.

_____

_____

_____

_____

_____

_____

_____

_____

_____

_____

_____

_____

_____

WHO IS CRAZY AUNT SUE WITH HAIR THAT IS BLUE?

_____

_____

_____

_____

_____

_____

_____

_____

_____

_____

_____

_____

_____

_____

WHAT DID THE FORTUNE TELLER SAY
TO THE GIRAFFE?

_____

_____

_____

_____

_____

_____

_____

_____

_____

_____

_____

_____

_____

TELL ABOUT THE PENGUIN WHO LEARNED TO FLY.

_____

_____

_____

_____

_____

_____

_____

_____

_____

_____

_____

_____

_____

_____

_____

DESCRIBE THE MOST DELICIOUS
FEAST IN THE WORLD.

TELL ABOUT A SUMMER TRIP TO THE NORTH POLE.

WHAT DID SANTA DO WHEN HE WAS A KID?

_____

_____

_____

_____

_____

_____

_____

_____

_____

_____

_____

_____

_____

_____

195

**YOU JUST TURNED DOWN $1 MILLION.
WHAT MADE YOU DO IT?**

_____

_____

_____

_____

_____

_____

_____

_____

_____

_____

_____

_____

_____

_____

_____

_____

_____

_____

**IF YOU COULD GO BACK IN TIME AND CHANGE ONE
EVENT IN HISTORY, WHAT WOULD IT BE?**

IF YOU COULD GAIN THREE TALENTS OR SKILLS OVERNIGHT, WHAT WOULD THEY BE?

_____

_____

_____

_____

_____

_____

_____

_____

_____

_____

_____

_____

_____

**WRITE A STORY ABOUT A PILOT WHO
WAS AFRAID OF FLYING.**

IMAGINE YOU ARE MOVING ACROSS THE COUNTRY. WHERE ARE YOU GOING AND WHAT WILL IT BE LIKE?

_____

_____

_____

_____

_____

_____

_____

_____

_____

_____

_____

_____

_____

_____

_____

_____

WHAT WOULD IT BE LIKE TO HAVE 25 SIBLINGS?

_____

_____

_____

_____

_____

_____

_____

_____

_____

_____

_____

_____

_____

_____

**IMAGINE YOU DISCOVERED A MYSTERIOUS OBJECT
WITH YOUR NAME ON IT. WHAT HAPPENS NEXT?**

_____

_____

_____

_____

_____

_____

_____

_____

_____

_____

_____

_____

_____

_____

_____

_____

DESCRIBE THE BEST SNOW DAY EVER.

_____

_____

_____

_____

_____

_____

_____

_____

_____

_____

_____

_____

_____

_____

_____

WHAT WOULD HAPPEN IF ALL CLOCKS SUDDENLY STOPPED?

_____

_____

_____

_____

_____

_____

_____

_____

_____

_____

_____

_____

_____

_____

IMAGINE YOU GET STUCK IN A STORE FOR MONTHS ON END. WHAT WOULD IT BE LIKE?

_____

_____

_____

_____

_____

_____

_____

_____

_____

_____

_____

_____

_____

_____

205

WRITE A STORY ABOUT A TIME YOU GOT CREDIT
FOR SOMETHING YOU DIDN'T DO.

_____

_____

_____

_____

_____

_____

_____

_____

_____

_____

_____

_____

_____

_____

DESCRIBE HOW YOU WON THE SCHOOL
TALENT SHOW.

_____

_____

_____

_____

_____

_____

_____

_____

_____

_____

_____

_____

_____

TELL A STORY ABOUT TWO PEOPLE WHO HAVE CONNECTED DREAMS.

_____

_____

_____

_____

_____

_____

_____

_____

_____

_____

_____

_____

_____

_____

WHAT IF YOU COULD RIDE ON RAINBOWS LIKE A ROLLERCOASTER?

WHAT IF BIRDS DELIVERED OUR PACKAGES?

_____

_____

_____

_____

_____

_____

_____

_____

_____

_____

_____

_____

_____

_____

_____

WHO SHOULD BE THE NEXT PRESIDENT?

_____

_____

_____

_____

_____

_____

_____

_____

_____

_____

_____

_____

_____

_____

IMAGINE YOU JUST RECEIVED AN ANONYMOUS LETTER WITH A WARNING. WHAT HAPPENS NEXT?

212

WHAT IF YOUR BEST FRIEND VANISHED INTO THIN AIR?

**WRITE A STORY ABOUT THE CRIMINAL
WHO COULD NEVER LIE.**

YOU MEET SOME NICE MONSTERS.
WHAT HAPPENS NEXT?

_____

_____

_____

_____

_____

_____

_____

_____

_____

_____

_____

_____

_____

_____

WHO WOULD YOU WANT TO SWAP LIVES WITH FOR A DAY, AND WHY?

216

WHAT IF IT NEVER GOT DARK OUTSIDE?

_____

_____

_____

_____

_____

_____

_____

_____

_____

_____

_____

_____

_____

_____

_____

WHAT IF SUMMER NEVER ENDED?

_____

_____

_____

_____

_____

_____

_____

_____

_____

_____

_____

_____

_____

_____

_____

218

WRITE ABOUT THE TIME THERE WAS AN
UNEXPECTED KNOCK ON YOUR WINDOW.

_____

_____

_____

_____

_____

_____

_____

_____

_____

_____

_____

_____

_____

IMAGINE YOU JUST DISCOVERED A NEW ANIMAL SPECIES. WHAT IS IT LIKE?

_____

_____

_____

_____

_____

_____

_____

_____

_____

_____

_____

_____

_____

_____

WHAT WOULD HAPPEN IF YOUR PET WAS IN CHARGE?

_____

_____

_____

_____

_____

_____

_____

_____

_____

_____

_____

_____

_____

_____

WRITE YOUR OWN STAND-UP COMEDY ROUTINE.

_____

_____

_____

_____

_____

_____

_____

_____

_____

_____

_____

_____

_____

_____

_____

WRITE A STORY ABOUT A BABYSITTER WHO DOESN'T
KNOW HOW TO TAKE CARE OF KIDS.

_____

_____

_____

_____

_____

_____

_____

_____

_____

_____

_____

_____

_____

_____

_____

223

WRITE A POEM ABOUT BACON.

WHAT'S THE REAL REASON CATS HATE WATER?

_____

_____

_____

_____

_____

_____

_____

_____

_____

_____

_____

_____

_____

WRITE A STORY ABOUT AN EPIC FOOD FIGHT.

_____

_____

_____

_____

_____

_____

_____

_____

_____

_____

_____

_____

_____

_____

_____

WHICH FICTIONAL CHARACTER IS THE
MOST LIKE YOU AND WHY?

_____

_____

_____

_____

_____

_____

_____

_____

_____

_____

_____

_____

_____

_____

_____

IF YOU MET A GENIE, WHAT WOULD BE YOUR THREE WISHES?

_____

_____

_____

_____

_____

_____

_____

_____

_____

_____

_____

_____

_____

_____

_____

WHAT IS THE BEST SMELL IN THE WORLD?

_____

_____

_____

_____

_____

_____

_____

_____

_____

_____

_____

_____

_____

_____

_____

WHAT DO DOGS DREAM ABOUT?

_____

_____

_____

_____

_____

_____

_____

_____

_____

_____

_____

_____

_____

_____

TELL A STORY ABOUT THE DINOSAUR WHO WANTED
TO BE A POLICE OFFICER.

_____

_____

_____

_____

_____

_____

_____

_____

_____

_____

_____

_____

_____

_____

WRITE A SONG ABOUT BRUSHING YOUR TEETH.

_____

_____

_____

_____

_____

_____

_____

_____

_____

_____

_____

_____

_____

_____

DESCRIBE A WORLD WHERE EVERYTHING
IS THE SAME COLOR.

_____

_____

_____

_____

_____

_____

_____

_____

_____

_____

_____

_____

_____

_____

_____

YOU SUDDENLY BECAME FAMOUS OVERNIGHT.
HOW DID IT HAPPEN?

_____

_____

_____

_____

_____

_____

_____

_____

_____

_____

_____

_____

_____

_____

_____

DESCRIBE THE WORLD'S MOST AMAZING
SECRET HIDEOUT.

_____

_____

_____

_____

_____

_____

_____

_____

_____

_____

_____

_____

_____

WHAT WOULD YOU DO IF YOU WOKE UP IN A PLACE WHERE NO ONE SPEAKS YOUR LANGUAGE?

WHAT IF THE GARBAGE MAN WAS
REALLY A SUPERHERO?

TELL A STORY ABOUT THE DAY YOUR STUFFED
ANIMAL CAME TO LIFE.

_____

_____

_____

_____

_____

_____

_____

_____

_____

_____

_____

_____

_____

_____

238

**IMAGINE YOU CAN SEE SOMETHING CRAZY—
BUT NO ONE ELSE SEES IT.**

239

**IF YOUR PARENTS SAID YES TO EVERYTHING
FOR A DAY, WHAT WOULD YOU DO?**

_____

_____

_____

_____

_____

_____

_____

_____

_____

_____

_____

_____

_____

_____

TELL A STORY ABOUT A WORM NAMED WALTER.

_____

_____

_____

_____

_____

_____

_____

_____

_____

_____

_____

_____

_____

_____

_____

_____

DESCRIBE THE DAY YOU WOKE UP AND DISCOVERED YOU'D TURNED BLUE.

_____

_____

_____

_____

_____

_____

_____

_____

_____

_____

_____

_____

_____

_____

242

IF YOU HAD TO RENAME THE COLOR GREEN,
WHAT WOULD YOU CALL IT?

_____

_____

_____

_____

_____

_____

_____

_____

_____

_____

_____

_____

_____

_____

IF YOU COULD ADD ANOTHER ROOM TO YOUR HOUSE, WHAT WOULD YOU PUT IN IT?

244

DESCRIBE THE DAY YOUR SECRET-AGENT PARENTS SAVED THE WORLD.

YOUR PARENTS JUST ANNOUNCED YOU'RE MOVING TO HAWAII. WHAT HAPPENS NEXT?

_____

_____

_____

_____

_____

_____

_____

_____

_____

_____

_____

_____

_____

_____

_____

WRITE ABOUT A TIME YOU ACCEPTED A CRAZY DARE.

_____

_____

_____

_____

_____

_____

_____

_____

_____

_____

_____

_____

_____

_____

YOU'RE ON A REMOTE ISLAND WITH NOTHING BUT A CHEESE GRATER. WHAT DO YOU DO WITH IT?

_____

_____

_____

_____

_____

_____

_____

_____

_____

_____

_____

_____

_____

_____

_____

_____

WRITE ABOUT THE TIME YOUR PET TARANTULA GOT LOST AT SCHOOL.

YOU WERE JUST PUT INTO A MAGICAL SLEEP. WHAT
WOULD HAVE TO HAPPEN TO BREAK THE SPELL?

_____

_____

_____

_____

_____

_____

_____

_____

_____

_____

_____

_____

_____

_____

_____

IF YOU COULD TRAIN YOUR PET TO HELP YOU DO
SOMETHING, WHAT WOULD YOU HAVE THEM DO?

_____

_____

_____

_____

_____

_____

_____

_____

_____

_____

_____

_____

_____

251

WOULD YOU EVER WANT TO CHANGE YOUR NAME?
WHAT WOULD YOU GO BY INSTEAD?

_____

_____

_____

_____

_____

_____

_____

_____

_____

_____

_____

_____

_____

_____

_____

YOU JUST SET A WORLD RECORD!
WHAT DID YOU DO?

_____

_____

_____

_____

_____

_____

_____

_____

_____

_____

_____

_____

_____

_____

DESCRIBE AN APRIL FOOL'S DAY PRANK
THAT WENT WRONG.

_____

_____

_____

_____

_____

_____

_____

_____

_____

_____

_____

_____

_____

_____

_____

_____

_____

INVENT A NEW SUBJECT TO STUDY AT SCHOOL.

_____

_____

_____

_____

_____

_____

_____

_____

_____

_____

_____

_____

_____

_____

_____

IF YOU COULD HAVE A CHARACTERISTIC OF AN ANIMAL—LIKE A SHARK'S FIN OR A GIRAFFE'S LONG NECK—WHAT WOULD YOU WANT?

_____

_____

_____

_____

_____

_____

_____

_____

_____

_____

_____

_____

_____

_____

DESCRIBE A BIKE THAT CAN GO ON WATER.

_____

_____

_____

_____

_____

_____

_____

_____

_____

_____

_____

_____

_____

_____

WHAT WOULD HAPPEN IF YOU WON EVERY GAME YOU EVER PLAYED?

DESCRIBE A WINDMILL THAT IS
POWERED BY LAUGHTER.

_____

_____

_____

_____

_____

_____

_____

_____

_____

_____

_____

_____

_____

_____

WRITE ABOUT A TIME YOU WENT THROUGH THE
CAR WASH WITH THE WINDOWS DOWN.

_____

_____

_____

_____

_____

_____

_____

_____

_____

_____

_____

_____

_____

IF YOU HAD YOUR DRIVER'S LICENSE, WHAT KIND OF CAR WOULD YOU DRIVE?

_____

_____

_____

_____

_____

_____

_____

_____

_____

_____

_____

_____

_____

_____

_____

_____

**DESCRIBE A WACKY FOOD COMBINATION THAT
SUDDENLY BECOMES POPULAR.**

_____

_____

_____

_____

_____

_____

_____

_____

_____

_____

_____

_____

_____

_____

_____

_____

262

IF YOU COULD GO BACK IN TIME AND CHANGE ONE THING THAT HAPPENED TO YOU THIS WEEK, WHAT WOULD IT BE?

_____

_____

_____

_____

_____

_____

_____

_____

_____

_____

_____

_____

_____

_____

YOU JUST FOUND OUT YOUR GREAT-GRANDPA WAS A FAMOUS HISTORICAL FIGURE. WHO WAS HE?

_____

_____

_____

_____

_____

_____

_____

_____

_____

_____

_____

_____

_____

_____

_____

_____

_____

YOU GET TO CREATE AN EPISODE OF *THE MAGIC SCHOOL BUS.* WHERE WOULD YOU GO, AND WHAT WOULD HAPPEN THERE?

_____

_____

_____

_____

_____

_____

_____

_____

_____

_____

_____

_____

_____

**WHAT IF BEES MADE SOMETHING BESIDES HONEY?
WHAT WOULD IT BE?**

_____

_____

_____

_____

_____

_____

_____

_____

_____

_____

_____

_____

_____

_____

DESCRIBE THE TIME YOU GOT CALLED INTO THE
PRINCIPAL'S OFFICE . . . AND LEFT WITH $100.

_____

_____

_____

_____

_____

_____

_____

_____

_____

_____

_____

_____

_____

_____

_____

WHAT WOULD HAPPEN IF PIGS WERE POLICE OFFICERS AND COWS WERE FIREMEN?

_____

_____

_____

_____

_____

_____

_____

_____

_____

_____

_____

_____

_____

_____

_____

_____

TELL ABOUT THE DAY YOU BABYSAT 597 GOATS.

_____

_____

_____

_____

_____

_____

_____

_____

_____

_____

_____

_____

_____

_____

_____

WHAT IF SPINACH TASTED LIKE CHOCOLATE AND CHOCOLATE TASTED LIKE SPINACH?

_____

_____

_____

_____

_____

_____

_____

_____

_____

_____

_____

_____

_____

_____

_____

_____

YOUR PARENTS SAY YOU HAVE TO GET A JOB.
WHERE WILL YOU WORK?

_____

_____

_____

_____

_____

_____

_____

_____

_____

_____

_____

_____

_____

_____

_____

DESCRIBE THE DAY YOU WENT ICE SKATING
ON CRUTCHES.

_____

_____

_____

_____

_____

_____

_____

_____

_____

_____

_____

_____

_____

_____

_____

IF SOMEONE HID A VIDEO CAMERA IN YOUR ROOM, WHAT'S THE FUNNIEST THING THEY'D SEE YOU DO?

_____

_____

_____

_____

_____

_____

_____

_____

_____

_____

_____

_____

_____

_____

_____

**WHAT'S THE STRANGEST THING YOU'VE EVER
SPENT YOUR OWN MONEY ON?**

IF EVERYONE STOPPED USING FORKS AND SPOONS,
WHAT WOULD BE THE HARDEST THING TO EAT?

_____

_____

_____

_____

_____

_____

_____

_____

_____

_____

_____

_____

_____

_____

_____

_____

275

IF ANIMALS COULD TALK, WHICH SPECIES DO
YOU THINK WOULD BE THE NICEST? SMARTEST?
MEANEST?

_____

_____

_____

_____

_____

_____

_____

_____

_____

_____

_____

_____

_____

_____

IF YOU COULD CHANGE YOUR NAME, WHAT WOULD YOU CHANGE IT TO? WHY?

_____

_____

_____

_____

_____

_____

_____

_____

_____

_____

_____

_____

_____

_____

_____

_____

WHAT WOULD YOU DO OR SAY IF THE WHOLE WORLD WAS WATCHING YOU ON LIVE TV FOR 60 SECONDS?

_____

_____

_____

_____

_____

_____

_____

_____

_____

_____

_____

_____

_____

_____

_____

IF YOU COULD BE A DESSERT, WHAT WOULD YOU BE?
WHY?

_____

_____

_____

_____

_____

_____

_____

_____

_____

_____

_____

_____

_____

_____

_____

WHAT'S THE CRAZIEST FACT YOU'VE EVER LEARNED?

WHAT WOULD IT BE LIKE TO HAVE 100 PETS?

_____

_____

_____

_____

_____

_____

_____

_____

_____

_____

_____

_____

_____

_____

_____

IF YOU WERE A PARENT, WHAT'S THE FUNNIEST NAME YOU COULD GIVE YOUR CHILD?

**WRITE A SHORT FAIRY TALE THAT TAKES PLACE
1,000 YEARS IN THE FUTURE.**

_____

_____

_____

_____

_____

_____

_____

_____

_____

_____

_____

_____

_____

_____

_____

_____

WHAT'S THE SILLIEST TALENT YOU HAVE?

_____

_____

_____

_____

_____

_____

_____

_____

_____

_____

_____

_____

_____

MAKE UP AN AMAZING ADVERTISEMENT
FOR TOILET PAPER.

INSTEAD OF BREADCRUMBS, WHAT DID HANSEL AND
GRETEL *REALLY* LEAVE AS A TRAIL TO FIND THEIR
WAY? WHAT HAPPENED?

_____

_____

_____

_____

_____

_____

_____

_____

_____

_____

_____

_____

_____

_____

_____

_____

IT'S APRIL FOOL'S DAY! WHAT WOULD YOU DO TO TRICK YOUR PARENTS?

_____

_____

_____

_____

_____

_____

_____

_____

_____

_____

_____

_____

_____

_____

_____

_____

287

WRITE A SONG ABOUT WHAT YOU ATE FOR LUNCH.

_____

_____

_____

_____

_____

_____

_____

_____

_____

_____

_____

_____

_____

_____

_____

288

WHAT WOULD HAPPEN AT THE WORLD'S BEST SUMMER CAMP?

_____

_____

_____

_____

_____

_____

_____

_____

_____

_____

_____

_____

_____

_____

_____

_____

DESCRIBE THE TIME YOU PLANNED THE WORLD'S BIGGEST WATER BALLOON FIGHT.

WHERE'S THE BEST PLACE TO HIDE DURING A GAME OF HIDE-AND-SEEK?

_____

_____

_____

_____

_____

_____

_____

_____

_____

_____

_____

_____

_____

_____

_____

WHAT IF YOUR GRANDMA WAS SECRETLY A SUPERHERO?

_____

_____

_____

_____

_____

_____

_____

_____

_____

_____

_____

_____

_____

_____

_____

_____

IF YOU WANTED TO MAKE EVERYONE YOU MEET LAUGH, HOW WOULD YOU DO IT?

_____

_____

_____

_____

_____

_____

_____

_____

_____

_____

_____

_____

_____

_____

IF YOU WERE AS SMALL AS AN ANT, HOW WOULD YOU DESCRIBE YOUR HOUSE?

WHAT'S YOUR MOST USELESS TALENT?

_____

_____

_____

_____

_____

_____

_____

_____

_____

_____

_____

_____

_____

_____

DESCRIBE THE COLORS OF THE RAINBOW
WITHOUT USING THEIR NAMES.

_____

_____

_____

_____

_____

_____

_____

_____

_____

_____

_____

_____

_____

_____

WHAT SMELL BRINGS BACK A STRONG MEMORY?
WHAT IS THE MEMORY?

_____

_____

_____

_____

_____

_____

_____

_____

_____

_____

_____

_____

_____

_____

_____

_____

**IF SOMEONE MADE A MOVIE ABOUT YOUR LIFE,
WHAT WOULD THEY CALL IT? WHY?**

**THERE WAS JUST A LOUD BANG DOWNSTAIRS.
WHAT HAPPENS NEXT?**

_____

_____

_____

_____

_____

_____

_____

_____

_____

_____

_____

_____

_____

_____

WHAT WOULD YOU DO IF YOU HAD SIX ARMS?

_____

_____

_____

_____

_____

_____

_____

_____

_____

_____

_____

_____

_____

_____

**IF YOU COULD OPEN A NEW RESTAURANT,
WHAT WOULD BE ON THE MENU?**

WRITE A LETTER TO YOUR FUTURE SELF.

_____

_____

_____

_____

_____

_____

_____

_____

_____

_____

_____

_____

_____

_____

ABOUT THE AUTHOR

Brooke is a word lover who can usually be found stocking up on expensive pints of ice cream, browsing the local bookstore, or hosting a dinner party. She's a California native who lives for sunny days, hiking, and weekend getaways.

ABOUT BUSHEL & PECK BOOKS

Bushel & Peck Books is a children's publishing house with a special mission. Through our Book-for-Book Promise™, we donate one book to kids in need for every book we sell. Our beautiful books are given to kids through schools, libraries, local neighborhoods, shelters, nonprofits, and also to many selfless organizations that are working hard to make a difference. So thank you for purchasing this book! Because of you, another book will make its way into the hands of a child who needs it most.

NOMINATE A SCHOOL OR ORGANIZATION TO RECEIVE FREE BOOKS

Do you know a school, library, or organization that could use some free books for their kids? We'd love to help! Please fill out the nomination form on our website (see below), and we'll do everything we can to make something happen.

www.bushelandpeckbooks.com/pages/
nominate-a-school-or-organization

If you liked this book, please leave a review online at your favorite retailer. Honest reviews spread the word about Bushel & Peck—and help us make better books, too!

Printed in the United States
by Baker & Taylor Publisher Services